CONFIDENT

A Journal for Athletes

Find Consistent Confidence in the Inconsistent World of Sports

Christen Shefchunas

I0570221

Confident – A Journal for Athletes

Find Consistent Confidence in the Inconsistent World of Sports

Author: Christen Shefchunas
Editor: Taylor Brien
Cover Design: Nicole Wurtele
Interior Layout: Michael Nicloy

ISBN: 979-8-9881891-8-3

PUBLISHED BY

CG SPORTS
PUBLISHING

AN IMPRINT OF
NICO 11 PUBLISHING & DESIGN
MUKWONAGO, WISCONSIN
MICHAEL NICLOY, PUBLISHER
www.nico11publishing.com

Quantity order requests can be emailed to:
mike@nico11publishing.com

Printed in The United States of America

Hard-working athletes often struggle to give themselves credit. No matter how well they perform, they have the mindset that if it's not perfect, it's not good enough. The one thing they might have done wrong gets all of their focus, instead of the 99 things they did well.

When athletes focus only on what they're not doing well, they don't feel that they're doing enough. They never feel prepared, which leads to struggling with confidence.

The goal of this journal is to practice giving yourself credit for at least one thing you do well each day. Write it under the Win of the Day. When you think of more than one, list the extras under More Good Stuff. The more you write down, the more reminders you will have that you have done the work to reach your goals.

And don't forget about mental wins. Write down at least one mental win of the day as well. These will be great reminders that you are mentally tough.

At the end of the week, recap all of the good stuff you did. There's also room to write three words that define who you were in those moments. These will be great reminders of who you are when you walk into competitions.

Each week of this journal begins with a reminder to help you find consistent confidence in the very inconsistent world of sports. Let that reminder guide you through the week.

You can get a more in-depth explanation of each reminder in the book *Confident. 52 Reminders for Consistent Confidence in the Inconsistent World of Sports*.

Some tips for using this journal:

- Be consistent. Do it every day.

- Be very specific about the moments that went well.

- Pay attention to the small moments. Those small moments add up to big confidence.

- Keep this journal somewhere close so you can write in it immediately after training. It's easy to forget the good stuff by the end of the day.

- Swimmers and runners, give yourself credit for effort, regardless of your times. (FYI, you're not going to be fast every day.)

- Create little goals for yourself, especially on the rough days. You want to walk out of each practice feeling accomplished.

- Before a competition, go back and read through your journal entries. Let them remind you that you have done the physical and mental work to be prepared to do extraordinary things.

1.

Confidence always revolves around truth.

This week:

Be honest with yourself. Be aware of what's going through your mind in training and at competitions.

Date _____

Win of the Day:

More Good Stuff:

Mental Wins:

Date _____

Win of the Day:

More Good Stuff:

Mental Wins:

Date _____

Win of the Day:

More Good Stuff:

Mental Wins:

Date _____

Win of the Day:

More Good Stuff:

Mental Wins:

Date _____

Win of the Day:

More Good Stuff:

Mental Wins:

Date _____

Win of the Day:

More Good Stuff:

Mental Wins:

Date_____

Biggest Wins of the Week:

Three words that define you in those moments:

_____

_____

_____

2.

"What ifs" can be scary, but they are totally normal. They don't mean you can't be confident.

This week:

Write a list of any "what ifs" and scary thoughts that pop up at practice or competitions.

Date _____

Win of the Day:

More Good Stuff:

Mental Wins:

Date _____

Win of the Day:

More Good Stuff:

Mental Wins:

Date _____

Win of the Day:

More Good Stuff:

Mental Wins:

Date _____

Win of the Day:

More Good Stuff:

Mental Wins:

Date _____

Win of the Day:

More Good Stuff:

Mental Wins:

Date _____

Win of the Day:

More Good Stuff:

Mental Wins:

Date_____

Biggest Wins of the Week:

Three words that define you in those moments:

_____

_____

_____

3.

Your confidence is your responsibility.

This week:

Pick one day to stay after practice to work on something you are struggling with.

Date _____

Win of the Day:

More Good Stuff:

Mental Wins:

Date _____

Win of the Day:

More Good Stuff:

Mental Wins:

Date _____

Win of the Day:

More Good Stuff:

Mental Wins:

Date _____

Win of the Day:

More Good Stuff:

Mental Wins:

Date _____

Win of the Day:

More Good Stuff:

Mental Wins:

Date _____

Win of the Day:

More Good Stuff:

Mental Wins:

Date_____

Biggest Wins of the Week:

Three words that define you in those moments:

_____

_____

_____

4.

Remember who you are in practice. That's you, even when you feel nervous.

This week:

Make a list of words that describe who you are in practice. Keep that list in a place where you can see it consistently.

Date _____

Win of the Day:

More Good Stuff:

Mental Wins:

Date _____

Win of the Day:

More Good Stuff:

Mental Wins:

Date _____

Win of the Day:

More Good Stuff:

Mental Wins:

Date _____

Win of the Day:

More Good Stuff:

Mental Wins:

Date _____

Win of the Day:

More Good Stuff:

Mental Wins:

Date _____

Win of the Day:

More Good Stuff:

Mental Wins:

Date_____

Biggest Wins of the Week:

Three words that define you in those moments:

_____

_____

_____

5.

You do not own a crystal ball. Trying to predict the future often leads to panic.

This week:

Catch yourself if you start predicting worst-case scenarios at practice or competitions and be intentional about getting your mind into the moment.

Date _____

Win of the Day:

More Good Stuff:

Mental Wins:

Date _____

Win of the Day:

More Good Stuff:

Mental Wins:

Date _____

Win of the Day:

More Good Stuff:

Mental Wins:

Date _____

Win of the Day:

More Good Stuff:

Mental Wins:

Date _____

Win of the Day:

More Good Stuff:

Mental Wins:

Date _____

Win of the Day:

More Good Stuff:

Mental Wins:

Date_____

Biggest Wins of the Week:

Three words that define you in those moments:

_____

_____

_____

6.

If you find yourself overthinking, get your mind out of the future and into the present.

This week:

Manage any overwhelming thoughts by talking them out or write them down on paper or on your phone.

Date _____

Win of the Day:

More Good Stuff:

Mental Wins:

Date _____

Win of the Day:

More Good Stuff:

Mental Wins:

Date _____

Win of the Day:

More Good Stuff:

Mental Wins:

Date _____

Win of the Day:

More Good Stuff:

Mental Wins:

Date _____

Win of the Day:

More Good Stuff:

Mental Wins:

Date _____

Win of the Day:

More Good Stuff:

Mental Wins:

Date_____

Biggest Wins of the Week:

Three words that define you in those moments:

_____

_____

_____

7.

Stop trying to con yourself into believing something that you don't. Speak truth.

This week:

Pay attention to what you tell yourself when you're feeling nervous. Do you believe it? If not, write down some new thoughts that you believe.

Date _____

Win of the Day:

More Good Stuff:

Mental Wins:

Date _____

Win of the Day:

More Good Stuff:

Mental Wins:

Date _____

Win of the Day:

More Good Stuff:

Mental Wins:

Date _____

Win of the Day:

More Good Stuff:

Mental Wins:

Date _____

Win of the Day:

More Good Stuff:

Mental Wins:

Date _____

Win of the Day:

More Good Stuff:

Mental Wins:

Date_____

Biggest Wins of the Week:

Three words that define you in those moments:

_____

_____

_____

8.

Every time you put in work, you put money in your bank. You're a millionaire.

This week:

When you feel like giving up, commit to putting a few more dollars in your bank.

Date _____

Win of the Day:

More Good Stuff:

Mental Wins:

Date _____

Win of the Day:

More Good Stuff:

Mental Wins:

Date _____

Win of the Day:

More Good Stuff:

Mental Wins:

Date _____

Win of the Day:

More Good Stuff:

Mental Wins:

Date _____

Win of the Day:

More Good Stuff:

Mental Wins:

Date _____

Win of the Day:

More Good Stuff:

Mental Wins:

Date_____

Biggest Wins of the Week:

Three words that define you in those moments:

_____

_____

_____

9.

Give yourself credit for the 99 things you're doing right.

This Week:

Commit to writing at least five good things that you do every day.

Date _____

Win of the Day:

More Good Stuff:

Mental Wins:

Date _____

Win of the Day:

More Good Stuff:

Mental Wins:

Date _____

Win of the Day:

More Good Stuff:

Mental Wins:

Date _____

Win of the Day:

More Good Stuff:

Mental Wins:

Date _____

Win of the Day:

More Good Stuff:

Mental Wins:

Date _____

Win of the Day:

More Good Stuff:

Mental Wins:

Date _____

Biggest Wins of the Week:

Three words that define you in those moments:

_____

_____

_____

10.

The more independent you are as an athlete, the more you will trust yourself. The more you trust yourself, the more powerful you will be.

This week:

Be intentional about trusting yourself.

Date _____

Win of the Day:

More Good Stuff:

Mental Wins:

Date _____

Win of the Day:

More Good Stuff:

Mental Wins:

Date _____

Win of the Day:

More Good Stuff:

Mental Wins:

Date _____

Win of the Day:

More Good Stuff:

Mental Wins:

Date _____

Win of the Day:

More Good Stuff:

Mental Wins:

Date _____

Win of the Day:

More Good Stuff:

Mental Wins:

Date_____

Biggest Wins of the Week:

Three words that define you in those moments:

_____

_____

_____

11.

Never allow comparing to take your "yay!" away.

This week:

Celebrate your accomplishments, regardless of what anyone else is doing. Write them in your journal!

Date _____

Win of the Day:

More Good Stuff:

Mental Wins:

Date _____

Win of the Day:

More Good Stuff:

Mental Wins:

Date _____

Win of the Day:

More Good Stuff:

Mental Wins:

Date _____

Win of the Day:

More Good Stuff:

Mental Wins:

Date _____

Win of the Day:

More Good Stuff:

Mental Wins:

Date _____

Win of the Day:

More Good Stuff:

Mental Wins:

Date_____

Biggest Wins of the Week:

Three words that define you in those moments:

_____

_____

_____

12.

The only things you can control are showing up and giving 100%. You know how to do that.

This week:

Commit to showing up and giving 100%, even when you feel nervous.

Date _____

Win of the Day:

More Good Stuff:

Mental Wins:

Date _____

Win of the Day:

More Good Stuff:

Mental Wins:

Date _____

Win of the Day:

More Good Stuff:

Mental Wins:

Date _____

Win of the Day:

More Good Stuff:

Mental Wins:

Date _____

Win of the Day:

More Good Stuff:

Mental Wins:

Date _____

Win of the Day:

More Good Stuff:

Mental Wins:

Date_____

Biggest Wins of the Week:

Three words that define you in those moments:

_____

_____

_____

13.

Failure is an inevitable part of sports. Take the time to learn from it.

This week:

Think about some disappointing performances. What can you learn from them?

Date _____

Win of the Day:

More Good Stuff:

Mental Wins:

Date _____

Win of the Day:

More Good Stuff:

Mental Wins:

Date _____

Win of the Day:

More Good Stuff:

Mental Wins:

Date _____

Win of the Day:

More Good Stuff:

Mental Wins:

Date _____

Win of the Day:

More Good Stuff:

Mental Wins:

Date _____

Win of the Day:

More Good Stuff:

Mental Wins:

Date_____

Biggest Wins of the Week:

Three words that define you in those moments:

_____

_____

_____

14.

Mentally tough is NOT sucking it up and pretending you're fine. Mentally tough is having the courage to be honest with yourself so you can help yourself.

This week:

Don't fake it. Write down 3 ways that you can be mentally tough.

Date _____

Win of the Day:

More Good Stuff:

Mental Wins:

Date _____

Win of the Day:

More Good Stuff:

Mental Wins:

Date _____

Win of the Day:

More Good Stuff:

Mental Wins:

Date _____

Win of the Day:

More Good Stuff:

Mental Wins:

Date _____

Win of the Day:

More Good Stuff:

Mental Wins:

Date _____

Win of the Day:

More Good Stuff:

Mental Wins:

Date_____

Biggest Wins of the Week:

Three words that define you in those moments:

_____

_____

_____

15.

You cannot predict the future, and it's time to accept that.

This week:

Accept that you don't know what's going to happen. Show up and give 100% anyway.

Date _____

Win of the Day:

More Good Stuff:

Mental Wins:

Date _____

Win of the Day:

More Good Stuff:

Mental Wins:

Date _____

Win of the Day:

More Good Stuff:

Mental Wins:

Date _____

Win of the Day:

More Good Stuff:

Mental Wins:

Date _____

Win of the Day:

More Good Stuff:

Mental Wins:

Date _____

Win of the Day:

More Good Stuff:

Mental Wins:

Date_____

Biggest Wins of the Week:

Three words that define you in those moments:

_____

_____

_____

16.

To get your mind present, answer the question, What do I know now?

This week:

Create a list of all the things that you know now.

Date _____

Win of the Day:

More Good Stuff:

Mental Wins:

Date _____

Win of the Day:

More Good Stuff:

Mental Wins:

Date _____

Win of the Day:

More Good Stuff:

Mental Wins:

Date _____

Win of the Day:

More Good Stuff:

Mental Wins:

Date _____

Win of the Day:

More Good Stuff:

Mental Wins:

Date _____

Win of the Day:

More Good Stuff:

Mental Wins:

Date_____

Biggest Wins of the Week:

Three words that define you in those moments:

_____

_____

_____

17.

It doesn't have to be perfect to be good.

This week:
If you are beating yourself up for a mistake or a bad play, repeat this statement.

Date _____

Win of the Day:

More Good Stuff:

Mental Wins:

Date _____

Win of the Day:

More Good Stuff:

Mental Wins:

Date _____

Win of the Day:

More Good Stuff:

Mental Wins:

Date _____

Win of the Day:

More Good Stuff:

Mental Wins:

Date _____

Win of the Day:

More Good Stuff:

Mental Wins:

Date _____

Win of the Day:

More Good Stuff:

Mental Wins:

Date_____

Biggest Wins of the Week:

Three words that define you in those moments:

_____

_____

_____

18.

Putting in hard work is not "just what you do." It's a choice. Your choices deserve credit.

This week:

Working hard is a choice. Pay attention to those choices you are making at practice and give yourself credit.

Date _____

Win of the Day:

More Good Stuff:

Mental Wins:

Date _____

Win of the Day:

More Good Stuff:

Mental Wins:

Date _____

Win of the Day:

More Good Stuff:

Mental Wins:

Date _____

Win of the Day:

More Good Stuff:

Mental Wins:

Date _____

Win of the Day:

More Good Stuff:

Mental Wins:

Date _____

Win of the Day:

More Good Stuff:

Mental Wins:

Date_____

Biggest Wins of the Week:

Three words that define you in those moments:

_____

_____

_____

19.

Your best is going to look different on different days.

This week:

Pay attention to the effort that you're giving, especially on the rough days when it's hard to find the good stuff.

Date _____

Win of the Day:

More Good Stuff:

Mental Wins:

Date _____

Win of the Day:

More Good Stuff:

Mental Wins:

Date _____

Win of the Day:

More Good Stuff:

Mental Wins:

Date _____

Win of the Day:

More Good Stuff:

Mental Wins:

Date _____

Win of the Day:

More Good Stuff:

Mental Wins:

Date _____

Win of the Day:

More Good Stuff:

Mental Wins:

Date_____

Biggest Wins of the Week:

Three words that define you in those moments:

_____

_____

_____

20.

Be consistent with your confidence journal.

This week:
Take a look back at what you´ve written so far.
It is all proof that you are doing the work to
reach your goals.

Date _____

Win of the Day:

More Good Stuff:

Mental Wins:

Date _____

Win of the Day:

More Good Stuff:

Mental Wins:

Date _____

Win of the Day:

More Good Stuff:

Mental Wins:

Date _____

Win of the Day:

More Good Stuff:

Mental Wins:

Date _____

Win of the Day:

More Good Stuff:

Mental Wins:

Date _____

Win of the Day:

More Good Stuff:

Mental Wins:

Date_____

Biggest Wins of the Week:

Three words that define you in those moments:

_____

_____

_____

21.

Journal your mental wins, too.

This week:

If you find yourself in a negative place, write down how you got yourself into a better place mentally.

Date _____

Win of the Day:

More Good Stuff:

Mental Wins:

Date _____

Win of the Day:

More Good Stuff:

Mental Wins:

Date _____

Win of the Day:

More Good Stuff:

Mental Wins:

Date _____

Win of the Day:

More Good Stuff:

Mental Wins:

Date _____

Win of the Day:

More Good Stuff:

Mental Wins:

Date _____

Win of the Day:

More Good Stuff:

Mental Wins:

Date_____

Biggest Wins of the Week:

Three words that define you in those moments:

_____

_____

_____

22.

Choose to be disciplined on days when you don't feel motivated.

This week:

Create a practice goal for yourself and commit to doing it everyday.

Date _____

Win of the Day:

More Good Stuff:

Mental Wins:

Date _____

Win of the Day:

More Good Stuff:

Mental Wins:

Date _____

Win of the Day:

More Good Stuff:

Mental Wins:

Date _____

Win of the Day:

More Good Stuff:

Mental Wins:

Date _____

Win of the Day:

More Good Stuff:

Mental Wins:

Date _____

Win of the Day:

More Good Stuff:

Mental Wins:

Date_____

Biggest Wins of the Week:

Three words that define you in those moments:

_____

_____

_____

23.

Being ready is not a feeling. It's a choice.

This week:
When you feel nervous, choose to go for it, even if you don't feel ready.

Date _____

Win of the Day:

More Good Stuff:

Mental Wins:

Date _____

Win of the Day:

More Good Stuff:

Mental Wins:

Date _____

Win of the Day:

More Good Stuff:

Mental Wins:

Date _____

Win of the Day:

More Good Stuff:

Mental Wins:

Date _____

Win of the Day:

More Good Stuff:

Mental Wins:

Date _____

Win of the Day:

More Good Stuff:

Mental Wins:

Date_____

Biggest Wins of the Week:

Three words that define you in those moments:

_____

_____

_____

24.

You don't have to think about your sport 24/7 to be great at your sport.

This week:

Find something that you enjoy doing that takes your mind off of your sport.

Date _____

Win of the Day:

More Good Stuff:

Mental Wins:

Date _____

Win of the Day:

More Good Stuff:

Mental Wins:

Date _____

Win of the Day:

More Good Stuff:

Mental Wins:

Date _____

Win of the Day:

More Good Stuff:

Mental Wins:

Date _____

Win of the Day:

More Good Stuff:

Mental Wins:

Date _____

Win of the Day:

More Good Stuff:

Mental Wins:

Date_____

Biggest Wins of the Week:

Three words that define you in those moments:

_____

_____

_____

25.

Get those heavy "have-to's" off of your shoulders.

This week:

What are some have-to's that you can take off your shoulders before walking into practice or a competition?

Date _____

Win of the Day:

More Good Stuff:

Mental Wins:

Date _____

Win of the Day:

More Good Stuff:

Mental Wins:

Date _____

Win of the Day:

More Good Stuff:

Mental Wins:

Date _____

Win of the Day:

More Good Stuff:

Mental Wins:

Date _____

Win of the Day:

More Good Stuff:

Mental Wins:

Date _____

Win of the Day:

More Good Stuff:

Mental Wins:

Date_____

Biggest Wins of the Week:

Three words that define you in those moments:

_____

_____

_____

26.

The better you handle the inevitable bad practices, the sooner you will bounce back.

This week:

Let yourself off the hook if you have a bad practice.

Date _____

Win of the Day:

More Good Stuff:

Mental Wins:

Date _____

Win of the Day:

More Good Stuff:

Mental Wins:

Date _____

Win of the Day:

More Good Stuff:

Mental Wins:

Date _____

Win of the Day:

More Good Stuff:

Mental Wins:

Date _____

Win of the Day:

More Good Stuff:

Mental Wins:

Date _____

Win of the Day:

More Good Stuff:

Mental Wins:

Date_____

Biggest Wins of the Week:

Three words that define you in those moments:

_____

_____

_____

27.

This is what you do. You know exactly what you're doing, even when you're nervous.

This week:

Trust that you know what you're doing.

Date _____

Win of the Day:

More Good Stuff:

Mental Wins:

Date _____

Win of the Day:

More Good Stuff:

Mental Wins:

Date _____

Win of the Day:

More Good Stuff:

Mental Wins:

Date _____

Win of the Day:

More Good Stuff:

Mental Wins:

Date _____

Win of the Day:

More Good Stuff:

Mental Wins:

Date _____

Win of the Day:

More Good Stuff:

Mental Wins:

Date_____

Biggest Wins of the Week:

Three words that define you in those moments:

_____

_____

_____

28.

Normalize the nerves.

This week:

Normalize some fears, doubts, or negative thoughts popping up when you feel the pressure at practice or a competition. No need to panic.

Date _____

Win of the Day:

More Good Stuff:

Mental Wins:

Date _____

Win of the Day:

More Good Stuff:

Mental Wins:

Date _____

Win of the Day:

More Good Stuff:

Mental Wins:

Date _____

Win of the Day:

More Good Stuff:

Mental Wins:

Date _____

Win of the Day:

More Good Stuff:

Mental Wins:

Date _____

Win of the Day:

More Good Stuff:

Mental Wins:

Date_____

Biggest Wins of the Week:

Three words that define you in those moments:

_____

_____

_____

29.

Don't self-sabotage by preparing yourself for a made-up story in your head.

This week:

Catch yourself if you're preparing for failure at practice or a competition.

Date _____

Win of the Day:

More Good Stuff:

Mental Wins:

Date _____

Win of the Day:

More Good Stuff:

Mental Wins:

Date _____

Win of the Day:

More Good Stuff:

Mental Wins:

Date _____

Win of the Day:

More Good Stuff:

Mental Wins:

Date _____

Win of the Day:

More Good Stuff:

Mental Wins:

Date _____

Win of the Day:

More Good Stuff:

Mental Wins:

Date_____

Biggest Wins of the Week:

Three words that define you in those moments:

_____

_____

_____

30.

Getting present is always an intentional decision.

This week:

Don´t get ahead of yourself. Take things one at a time.

Date _____

Win of the Day:

More Good Stuff:

Mental Wins:

Date _____

Win of the Day:

More Good Stuff:

Mental Wins:

Date _____

Win of the Day:

More Good Stuff:

Mental Wins:

Date _____

Win of the Day:

More Good Stuff:

Mental Wins:

Date _____

Win of the Day:

More Good Stuff:

Mental Wins:

Date _____

Win of the Day:

More Good Stuff:

Mental Wins:

Date_____

Biggest Wins of the Week:

Three words that define you in those moments:

_____

_____

_____

31.

You don't have to feel perfect to perform well.

This week:

Journal the moments when you don't feel perfect, but you surprised yourself and performed better than expected.

Date _____

Win of the Day:

More Good Stuff:

Mental Wins:

Date _____

Win of the Day:

More Good Stuff:

Mental Wins:

Date _____

Win of the Day:

More Good Stuff:

Mental Wins:

Date _____

Win of the Day:

More Good Stuff:

Mental Wins:

Date _____

Win of the Day:

More Good Stuff:

Mental Wins:

Date _____

Win of the Day:

More Good Stuff:

Mental Wins:

Date_____

Biggest Wins of the Week:

Three words that define you in those moments:

_____

_____

_____

32.

Don't get caught in the comparison trap. Get your focus off of others and back to yourself.

This week:

List some moments where you found yourself comparing, but you got your focus back to you.

Date _____

Win of the Day:

More Good Stuff:

Mental Wins:

Date _____

Win of the Day:

More Good Stuff:

Mental Wins:

Date _____

Win of the Day:

More Good Stuff:

Mental Wins:

Date _____

Win of the Day:

More Good Stuff:

Mental Wins:

Date _____

Win of the Day:

More Good Stuff:

Mental Wins:

Date _____

Win of the Day:

More Good Stuff:

Mental Wins:

Date_____

Biggest Wins of the Week:

Three words that define you in those moments:

_____

_____

_____

33.

Validate yourself.

This week:

Stop looking to others to validate you. Write down a moment that you gave yourself credit when you didn't hear anyone else say, good job.

Date _____

Win of the Day:

More Good Stuff:

Mental Wins:

Date _____

Win of the Day:

More Good Stuff:

Mental Wins:

Date _____

Win of the Day:

More Good Stuff:

Mental Wins:

Date _____

Win of the Day:

More Good Stuff:

Mental Wins:

Date _____

Win of the Day:

More Good Stuff:

Mental Wins:

Date _____

Win of the Day:

More Good Stuff:

Mental Wins:

Date_____

Biggest Wins of the Week:

Three words that define you in those moments:

_____

_____

_____

34.

Pay attention to what works and what doesn't work for you.

This week:

What is working well for you right now? What is one thing that might not be working for you? Edit or delete what isn't working for you.

Date _____

Win of the Day:

More Good Stuff:

Mental Wins:

Date _____

Win of the Day:

More Good Stuff:

Mental Wins:

Date _____

Win of the Day:

More Good Stuff:

Mental Wins:

Date _____

Win of the Day:

More Good Stuff:

Mental Wins:

Date _____

Win of the Day:

More Good Stuff:

Mental Wins:

Date _____

Win of the Day:

More Good Stuff:

Mental Wins:

Date_____

Biggest Wins of the Week:

Three words that define you in those moments:

_____

_____

_____

35.

You'll never know how good you can be if you're not willing to take risks.

This week:
Take at least one risk every day.

Date _____

Win of the Day:

More Good Stuff:

Mental Wins:

Risk of the Day:

Date _____

Win of the Day:

More Good Stuff:

Mental Wins:

Risk of the Day:

Date _____

Win of the Day:

More Good Stuff:

Mental Wins:

Risk of the Day:

Date _____

Win of the Day:

More Good Stuff:

Mental Wins:

Risk of the Day:

Date _____

Win of the Day:

More Good Stuff:

Mental Wins:

Risk of the Day:

Date _____

Win of the Day:

More Good Stuff:

Mental Wins:

Risk of the Day:

Date_____

Biggest Wins of the Week:

Three words that define you in those moments:

_____

_____

_____

36.

You don't have to be in a perfect place mentally to be in a good place.

This week:

If you feel nervous or have doubts, remind yourself that you're still mentally tough.

Date _____

Win of the Day:

More Good Stuff:

Mental Wins:

Date _____

Win of the Day:

More Good Stuff:

Mental Wins:

Date _____

Win of the Day:

More Good Stuff:

Mental Wins:

Date _____

Win of the Day:

More Good Stuff:

Mental Wins:

Date _____

Win of the Day:

More Good Stuff:

Mental Wins:

Date _____

Win of the Day:

More Good Stuff:

Mental Wins:

Date_____

Biggest Wins of the Week:

Three words that define you in those moments:

_____

_____

_____

37.

Don't panic after a bad competition.

This week:

Remember that every athlete in the world has bad competitions. It doesn't change who you are.

Date _____

Win of the Day:

More Good Stuff:

Mental Wins:

Date _____

Win of the Day:

More Good Stuff:

Mental Wins:

Date _____

Win of the Day:

More Good Stuff:

Mental Wins:

Date _____

Win of the Day:

More Good Stuff:

Mental Wins:

Date _____

Win of the Day:

More Good Stuff:

Mental Wins:

Date _____

Win of the Day:

More Good Stuff:

Mental Wins:

Date_____

Biggest Wins of the Week:

Three words that define you in those moments:

_____

_____

_____

38.

The more stubborn you are, the more you will want to control things you cannot control. Get your focus back to you.

This week:

Control what you can control.

Date _____

Win of the Day:

More Good Stuff:

Mental Wins:

Date _____

Win of the Day:

More Good Stuff:

Mental Wins:

Date _____

Win of the Day:

More Good Stuff:

Mental Wins:

Date _____

Win of the Day:

More Good Stuff:

Mental Wins:

Date _____

Win of the Day:

More Good Stuff:

Mental Wins:

Date _____

Win of the Day:

More Good Stuff:

Mental Wins:

Date_____

Biggest Wins of the Week:

Three words that define you in those moments:

_____

_____

_____

39.

It is your responsibility to surround yourself with the right people and to walk away from others.

This week:

Be wise about who you spend your time with.

Date _____

Win of the Day:

More Good Stuff:

Mental Wins:

Date _____

Win of the Day:

More Good Stuff:

Mental Wins:

Date _____

Win of the Day:

More Good Stuff:

Mental Wins:

Date _____

Win of the Day:

More Good Stuff:

Mental Wins:

Date _____

Win of the Day:

More Good Stuff:

Mental Wins:

Date _____

Win of the Day:

More Good Stuff:

Mental Wins:

Date_____

Biggest Wins of the Week:

Three words that define you in those moments:

_____

_____

_____

40.

If you're trying not to think about it, you're already thinking about it. Admit it, so you can do something about it.

This week:

Don't try to block out your thoughts. Be honest with yourself.

Date _____

Win of the Day:

More Good Stuff:

Mental Wins:

Date _____

Win of the Day:

More Good Stuff:

Mental Wins:

Date _____

Win of the Day:

More Good Stuff:

Mental Wins:

Date _____

Win of the Day:

More Good Stuff:

Mental Wins:

Date _____

Win of the Day:

More Good Stuff:

Mental Wins:

Date _____

Win of the Day:

More Good Stuff:

Mental Wins:

Date_____

Biggest Wins of the Week:

Three words that define you in those moments:

_____

_____

_____

41.

Your mental health must always be your priority.

This week:

Make a list of the ways you are going to take care of your mental health.

Date _____

Win of the Day:

More Good Stuff:

Mental Wins:

Date _____

Win of the Day:

More Good Stuff:

Mental Wins:

Date _____

Win of the Day:

More Good Stuff:

Mental Wins:

Date _____

Win of the Day:

More Good Stuff:

Mental Wins:

Date _____

Win of the Day:

More Good Stuff:

Mental Wins:

Date _____

Win of the Day:

More Good Stuff:

Mental Wins:

Date_____

Biggest Wins of the Week:

Three words that define you in those moments:

_____

_____

_____

42.

You know how to do hard.

This week:
Do 3 hard things that get you closer to your goals.

Date _____

Win of the Day:

More Good Stuff:

Mental Wins:

Date _____

Win of the Day:

More Good Stuff:

Mental Wins:

Date _____

Win of the Day:

More Good Stuff:

Mental Wins:

Date _____

Win of the Day:

More Good Stuff:

Mental Wins:

Date _____

Win of the Day:

More Good Stuff:

Mental Wins:

Date _____

Win of the Day:

More Good Stuff:

Mental Wins:

Date_____

Biggest Wins of the Week:

Three words that define you in those moments:

_____

_____

_____

43.

You can always come back from a disappointing start.

This week:

Think back to a practice or competition where it didn't start as well as you had hoped. How did you bounce back from it?

Date _____

Win of the Day:

More Good Stuff:

Mental Wins:

Date _____

Win of the Day:

More Good Stuff:

Mental Wins:

Date _____

Win of the Day:

More Good Stuff:

Mental Wins:

Date _____

Win of the Day:

More Good Stuff:

Mental Wins:

Date _____

Win of the Day:

More Good Stuff:

Mental Wins:

Date _____

Win of the Day:

More Good Stuff:

Mental Wins:

Date_____

Biggest Wins of the Week:

Three words that define you in those moments:

_____

_____

_____

44.

Consistently remind yourself of who you are.

This week:

Write some words to define who you are when you're "playing like yourself" or "racing like you."

Date _____

Win of the Day:

More Good Stuff:

Mental Wins:

Date _____

Win of the Day:

More Good Stuff:

Mental Wins:

Date _____

Win of the Day:

More Good Stuff:

Mental Wins:

Date _____

Win of the Day:

More Good Stuff:

Mental Wins:

Date _____

Win of the Day:

More Good Stuff:

Mental Wins:

Date _____

Win of the Day:

More Good Stuff:

Mental Wins:

Date_____

Biggest Wins of the Week:

Three words that define you in those moments:

_____

_____

_____

45.

You will get nervous, but you can control it.

This week:

Be aware when your mind is wandering into scary thoughts. Take control and get into the present.

Date _____

Win of the Day:

More Good Stuff:

Mental Wins:

Date _____

Win of the Day:

More Good Stuff:

Mental Wins:

Date _____

Win of the Day:

More Good Stuff:

Mental Wins:

Date _____

Win of the Day:

More Good Stuff:

Mental Wins:

Date _____

Win of the Day:

More Good Stuff:

Mental Wins:

Date _____

Win of the Day:

More Good Stuff:

Mental Wins:

Date_____

Biggest Wins of the Week:

Three words that define you in those moments:

_____

_____

_____

46.

Your confidence is always there, even when you can't feel it.

This week:

Write down some of your more confident moments in practices or competitions. That's your confidence at all times.

Date _____

Win of the Day:

More Good Stuff:

Mental Wins:

Date _____

Win of the Day:

More Good Stuff:

Mental Wins:

Date _____

Win of the Day:

More Good Stuff:

Mental Wins:

Date _____

Win of the Day:

More Good Stuff:

Mental Wins:

Date _____

Win of the Day:

More Good Stuff:

Mental Wins:

Date _____

Win of the Day:

More Good Stuff:

Mental Wins:

Date_____

Biggest Wins of the Week:

Three words that define you in those moments:

_____

_____

_____

47.

You can be real about your feelings and still be positive.

This week:

Be positive without faking it.

Date _____

Win of the Day:

More Good Stuff:

Mental Wins:

Date _____

Win of the Day:

More Good Stuff:

Mental Wins:

Date _____

Win of the Day:

More Good Stuff:

Mental Wins:

Date _____

Win of the Day:

More Good Stuff:

Mental Wins:

Date _____

Win of the Day:

More Good Stuff:

Mental Wins:

Date _____

Win of the Day:

More Good Stuff:

Mental Wins:

Date_____

Biggest Wins of the Week:

Three words that define you in those moments:

_____

_____

_____

48.

Before competitions, do the work to mentally prepare yourself.

This week:

Look back at what you´ve written in this journal. Use these reminders to prepare yourself mentally.

Date _____

Win of the Day:

More Good Stuff:

Mental Wins:

Date _____

Win of the Day:

More Good Stuff:

Mental Wins:

Date _____

Win of the Day:

More Good Stuff:

Mental Wins:

Date _____

Win of the Day:

More Good Stuff:

Mental Wins:

Date _____

Win of the Day:

More Good Stuff:

Mental Wins:

Date _____

Win of the Day:

More Good Stuff:

Mental Wins:

Date_____

Biggest Wins of the Week:

Three words that define you in those moments:

_____

_____

_____

49.

It is your responsibility to protect your peace.

This week:

Write down the things that you should do to protect your peace before competitions.

Date _____

Win of the Day:

More Good Stuff:

Mental Wins:

Date _____

Win of the Day:

More Good Stuff:

Mental Wins:

Date _____

Win of the Day:

More Good Stuff:

Mental Wins:

Date _____

Win of the Day:

More Good Stuff:

Mental Wins:

Date _____

Win of the Day:

More Good Stuff:

Mental Wins:

Date _____

Win of the Day:

More Good Stuff:

Mental Wins:

Date_____

Biggest Wins of the Week:

Three words that define you in those moments:

_____

_____

_____

50.

You have no control over anyone else.
Good news — they have no control over
you, either.

This week:

Show up and do your thing!

Date _____

Win of the Day:

More Good Stuff:

Mental Wins:

Date _____

Win of the Day:

More Good Stuff:

Mental Wins:

Date _____

Win of the Day:

More Good Stuff:

Mental Wins:

Date _____

Win of the Day:

More Good Stuff:

Mental Wins:

Date _____

Win of the Day:

More Good Stuff:

Mental Wins:

Date _____

Win of the Day:

More Good Stuff:

Mental Wins:

Date_____

Biggest Wins of the Week:

Three words that define you in those moments:

_____

_____

_____

51.

Stop beating yourself up for not being perfect.

This week:

Accept that you´re not going to be perfect. Give yourself credit for giving your best.

Date _____

Win of the Day:

More Good Stuff:

Mental Wins:

Date _____

Win of the Day:

More Good Stuff:

Mental Wins:

Date _____

Win of the Day:

More Good Stuff:

Mental Wins:

Date _____

Win of the Day:

More Good Stuff:

Mental Wins:

Date _____

Win of the Day:

More Good Stuff:

Mental Wins:

Date _____

Win of the Day:

More Good Stuff:

Mental Wins:

Date_____

Biggest Wins of the Week:

Three words that define you in those moments:

_____

_____

_____

52.

**Confidence takes work.
Do the work.**

This week:
Continue to DO THE WORK.

Date _____

Win of the Day:

More Good Stuff:

Mental Wins:

Date _____

Win of the Day:

More Good Stuff:

Mental Wins:

Date _____

Win of the Day:

More Good Stuff:

Mental Wins:

Date _____

Win of the Day:

More Good Stuff:

Mental Wins:

Date _____

Win of the Day:

More Good Stuff:

Mental Wins:

Date _____

Win of the Day:

More Good Stuff:

Mental Wins:

Date_____

Biggest Wins of the Week:

Three words that define you in those moments:

_____

_____

_____

Christen Shefchunas is a Professional Confidence Coach who works with World Record Holders, Olympians, and NCAA Champions.

She is a former All-American Swimmer at the University of Tennessee and coached for 16 years, spending time as an assistant coach at Michigan State and SMU, and Head Coach at the University of Miami.

During her time as a coach, Christen watched too many athletes miss out on their potential because of their lack of confidence. Realizing that there was a significant lack of resources for these athletes, Christen left her coaching career and started Coach Christen, a business focused on helping athletes handle the pressure and build their confidence.

She works one-on-one as a confidence coach with some of the best athletes in the world and she is a sought after speaker, speaking to teams, athletes, coaches, parents, and business leaders about how to handle the pressure and how to build consistent confidence in the inconsistent world of sports.